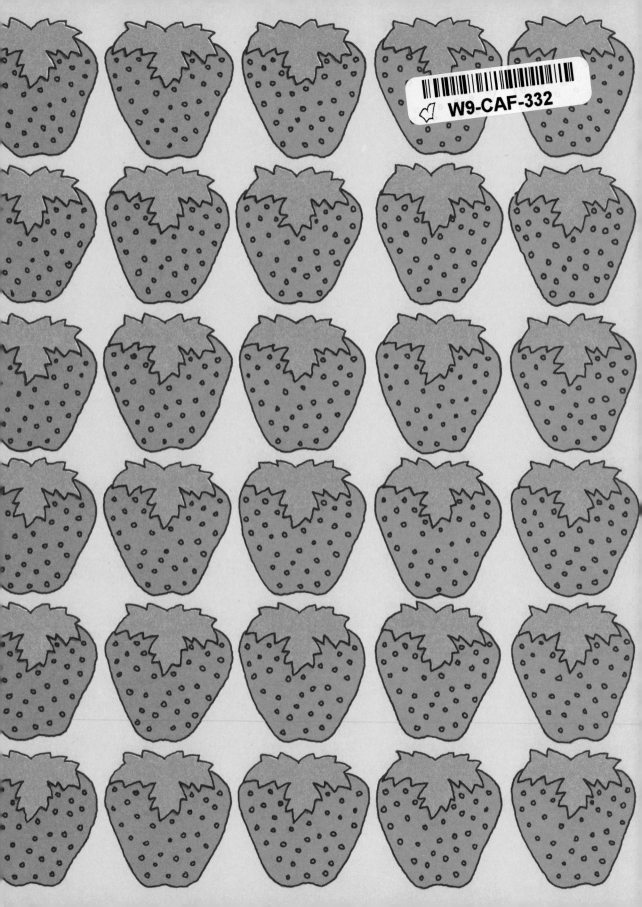

W9-CAF-332

this
strawberry library
of first learning
book
belongs to

*this book
is for
Bobbie
and
Player
and
Eric
and
Peter
and
Jay*

Copyright © 1975 by One Strawberry, Inc.
All rights reserved
Printed in the United States of America
Library of Congress Catalog Card Number: 74-81376
ISBN: Trade 0-88470-008-9, Library 0-88470-009-7

Weekly Reader Books Edition

things that go

by Richard Hefter

a strawberry book®

cars
and trucks
and
things that go
on land

A tow truck towing a truck.

A boy towing a wagon.

A car towing a boat.

cab

trailer

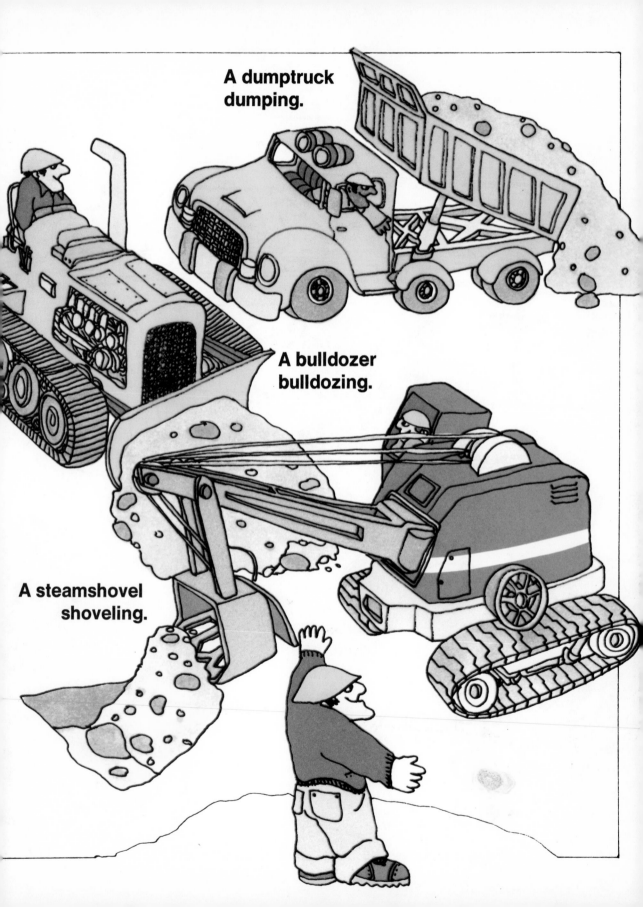

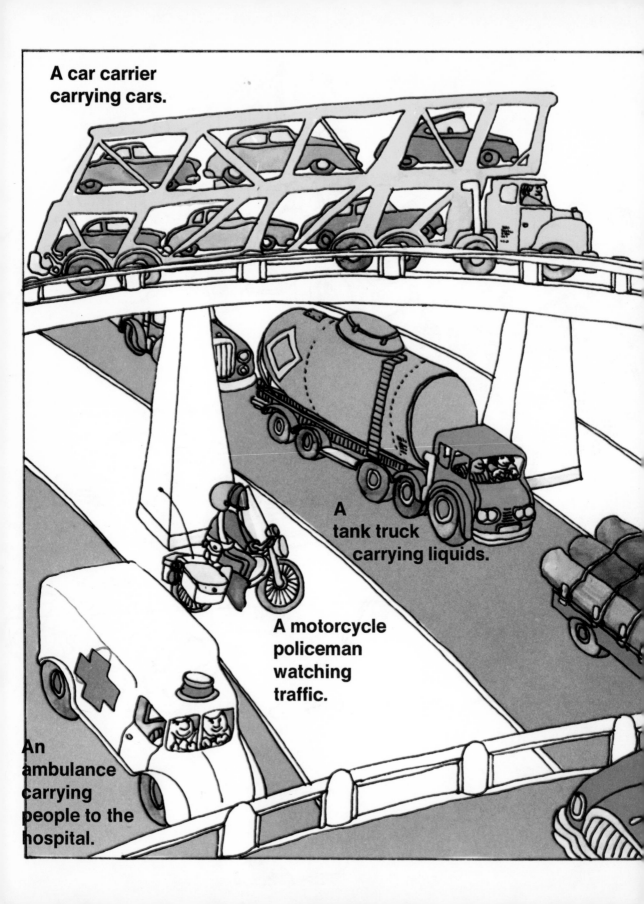

A car carrier carrying cars.

A tank truck carrying liquids.

A motorcycle policeman watching traffic.

An ambulance carrying people to the hospital.

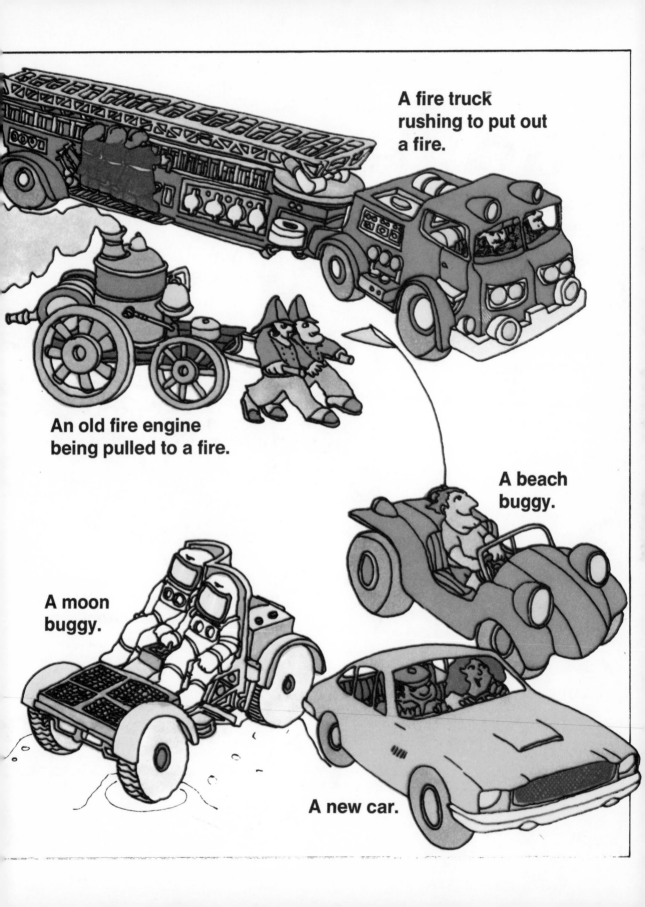

A fire truck
rushing to put out
a fire.

An old fire engine
being pulled to a fire.

A beach
buggy.

A moon
buggy.

A new car.

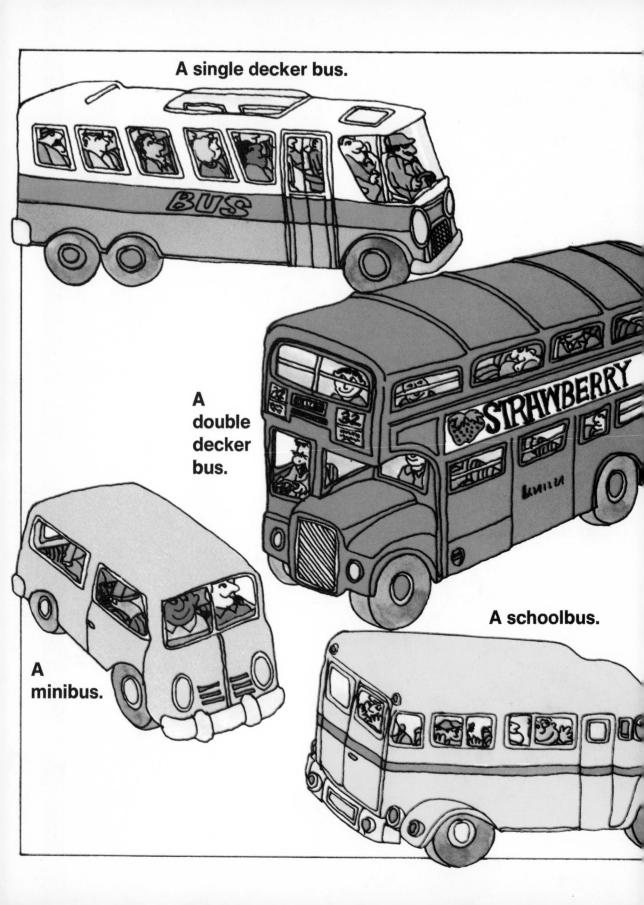

A single decker bus.

A double decker bus.

A minibus.

A schoolbus.

Racing cars go very fast.

A bicycle has two wheels.

A tricycle has three wheels.

A unicycle has one wheel.

A pair of roller skates.

A scooter.

A wagon.

trains
and trolleys
and
things that go
on tracks

A very old steam locomotive.

A new steam locomotive.

Some funicular railways run uphill.

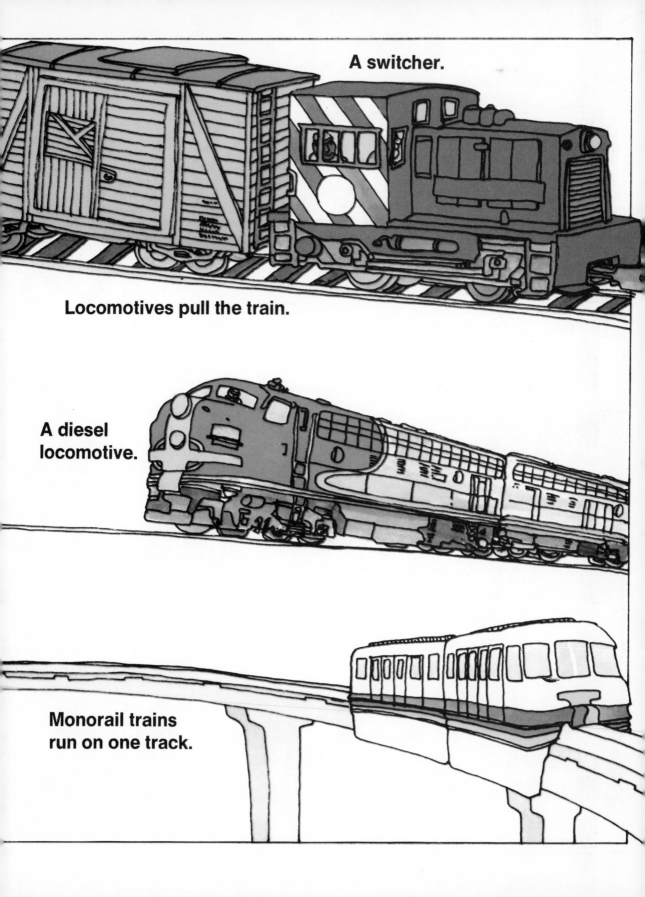

A switcher.

Locomotives pull the train.

A diesel
locomotive.

Monorail trains
run on one track.

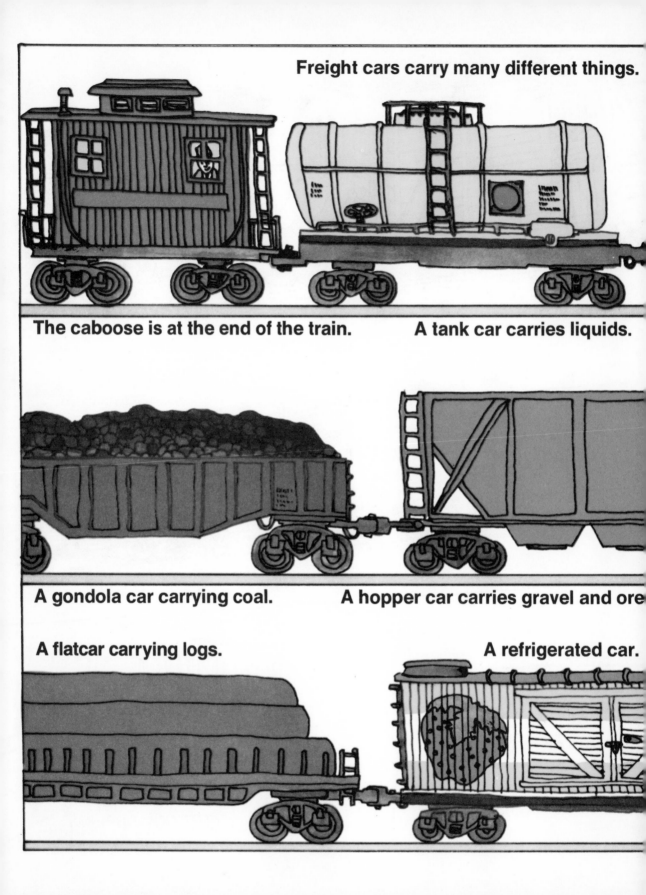

Freight cars carry many different things.

The caboose is at the end of the train.

A tank car carries liquids.

A gondola car carrying coal.

A hopper car carries gravel and ore

A flatcar carrying logs.

A refrigerated car.

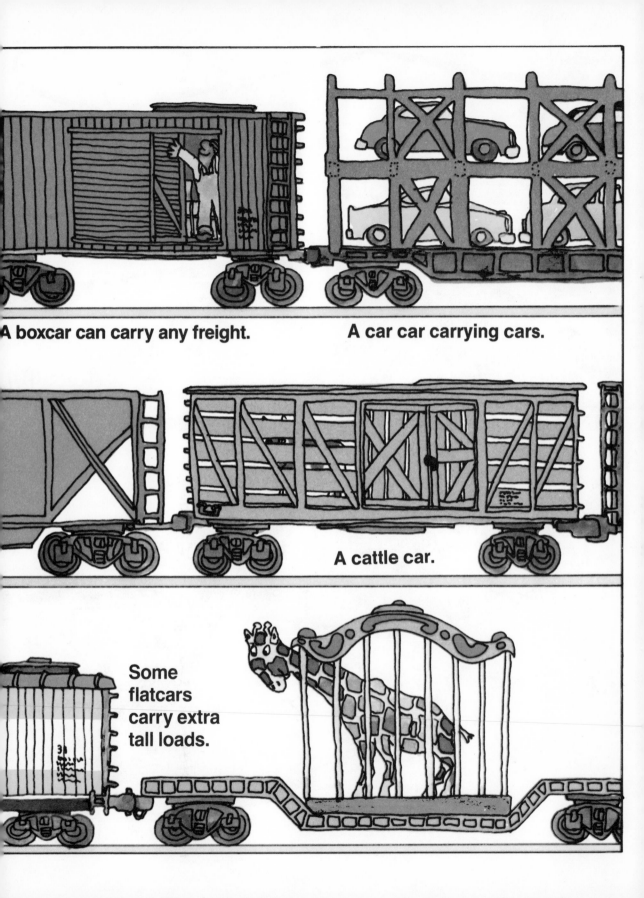

A boxcar can carry any freight.

A car car carrying cars.

A cattle car.

Some
flatcars
carry extra
tall loads.

Trains go everywhere on tracks.

An electric passenger train gets its power from overhead lines.

A trolley rides along the street on tracks.

Subways run underground on tracks.

planes and rockets and things that go in the air and space

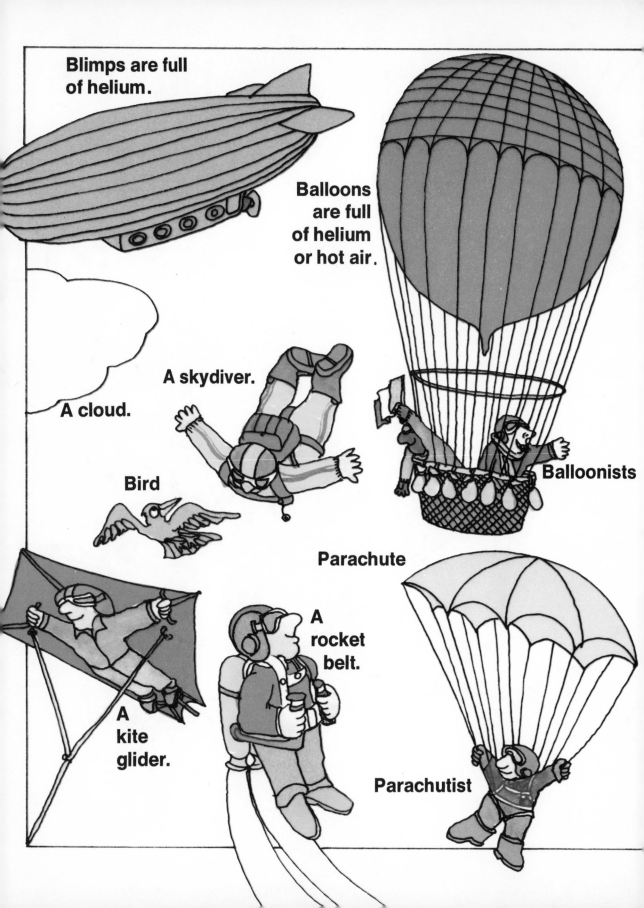

Blimps are full of helium.

Balloons are full of helium or hot air.

A cloud.

A skydiver.

Bird

Balloonists

Parachute

A rocket belt.

A kite glider.

Parachutist

A biplane
has two wings.

A helicopter
has no wings.

A triplane
has three
wings.

Pilot

Seaplanes
land on the water.

Pontoons

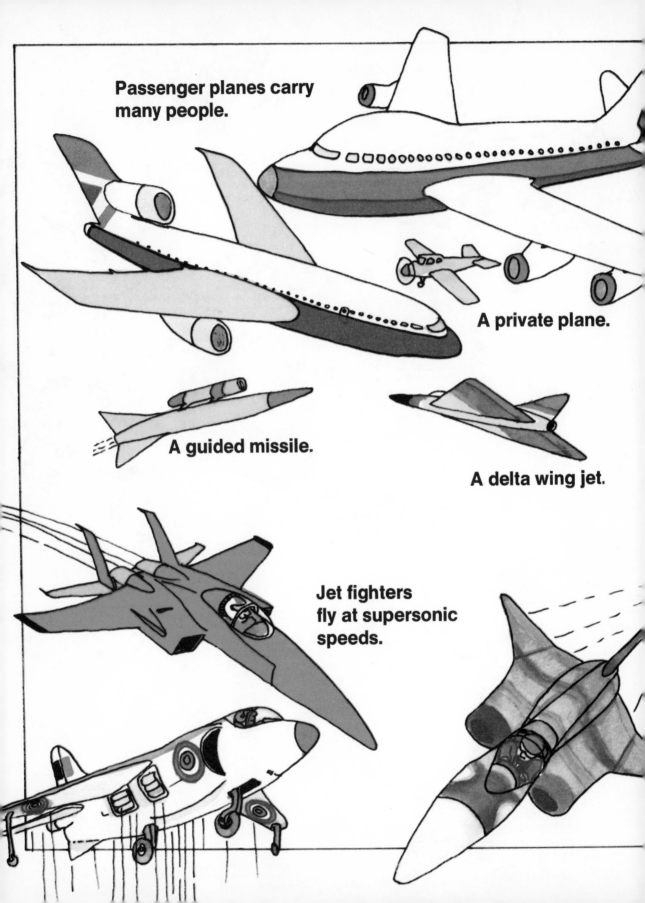

Passenger planes carry many people.

A private plane.

A guided missile.

A delta wing jet.

Jet fighters fly at supersonic speeds.

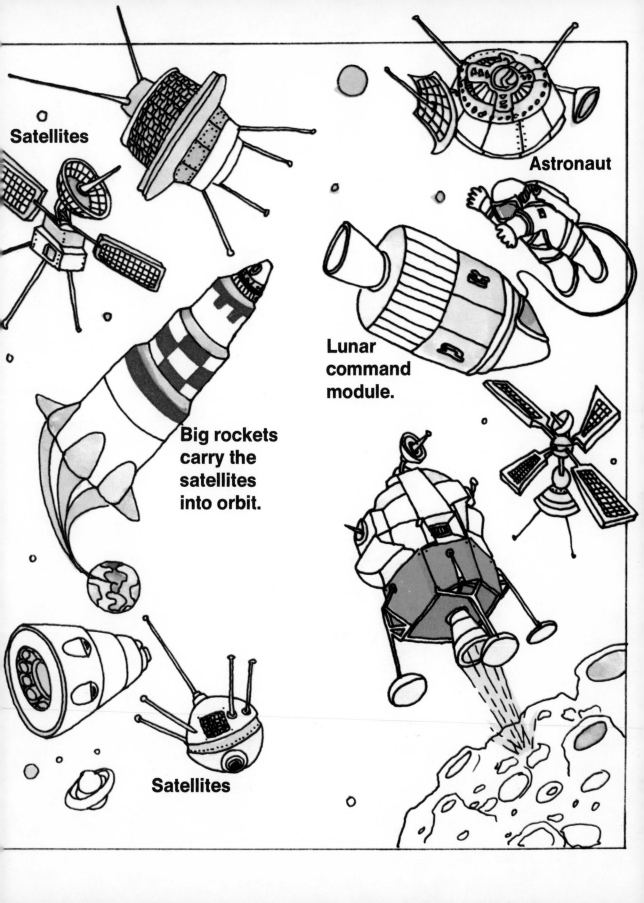

Satellites

Astronaut

Lunar command module.

Big rockets carry the satellites into orbit.

Satellites

ships
and boats
and
things that go
in the water

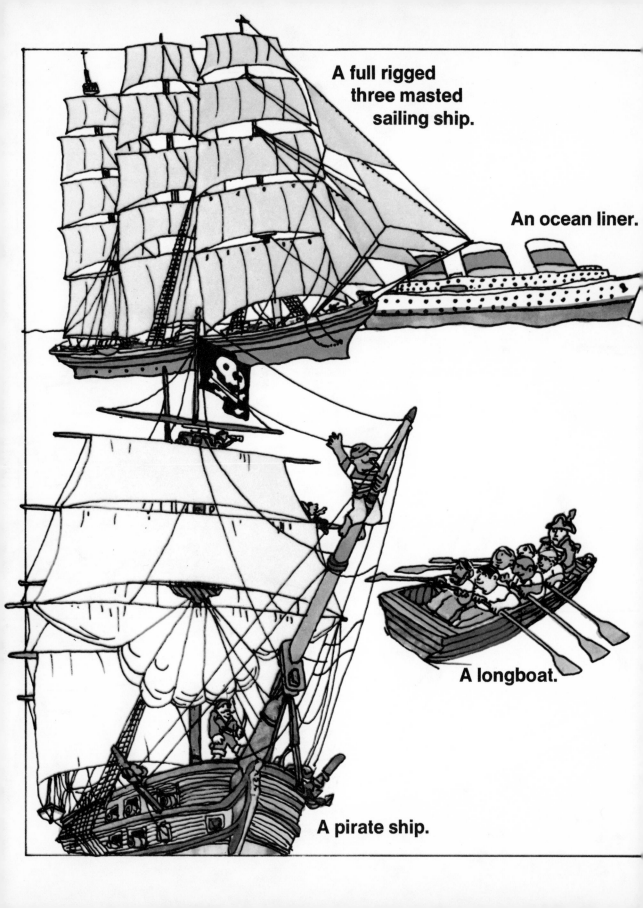

A full rigged
three masted
sailing ship.

An ocean liner.

A longboat.

A pirate ship.

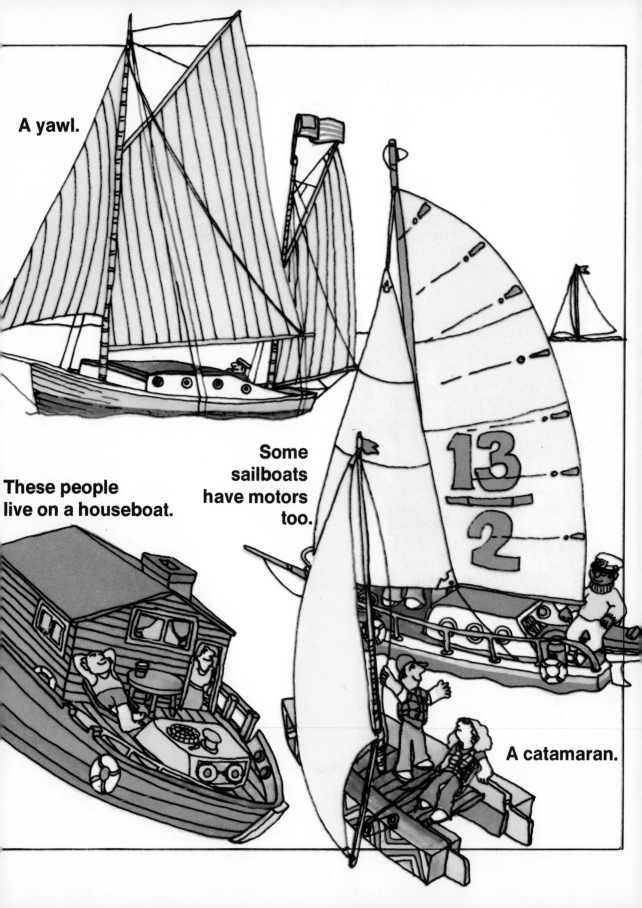

A yawl.

These people
live on a houseboat.

Some
sailboats
have motors
too.

13
2

A catamaran.

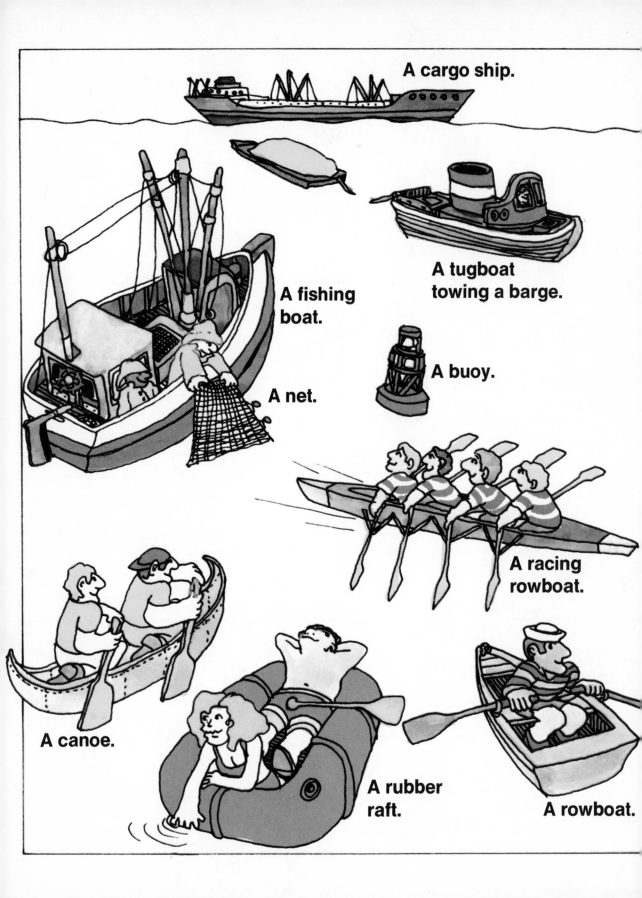

A cargo ship.

A fishing boat.

A tugboat towing a barge.

A buoy.

A net.

A racing rowboat.

A canoe.

A rubber raft.

A rowboat.

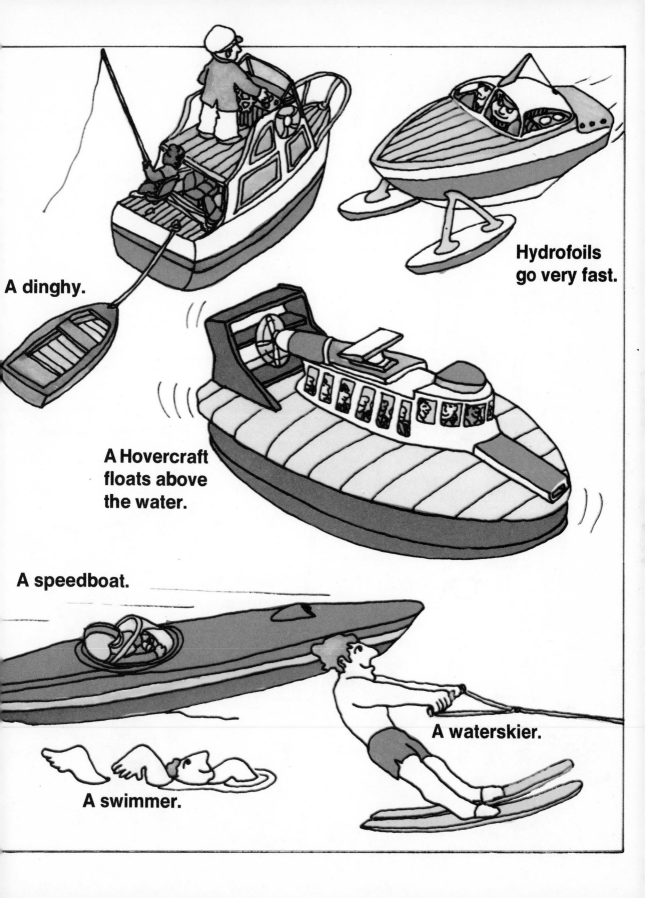

A dinghy.

Hydrofoils go very fast.

A Hovercraft floats above the water.

A speedboat.

A waterskier.

A swimmer.

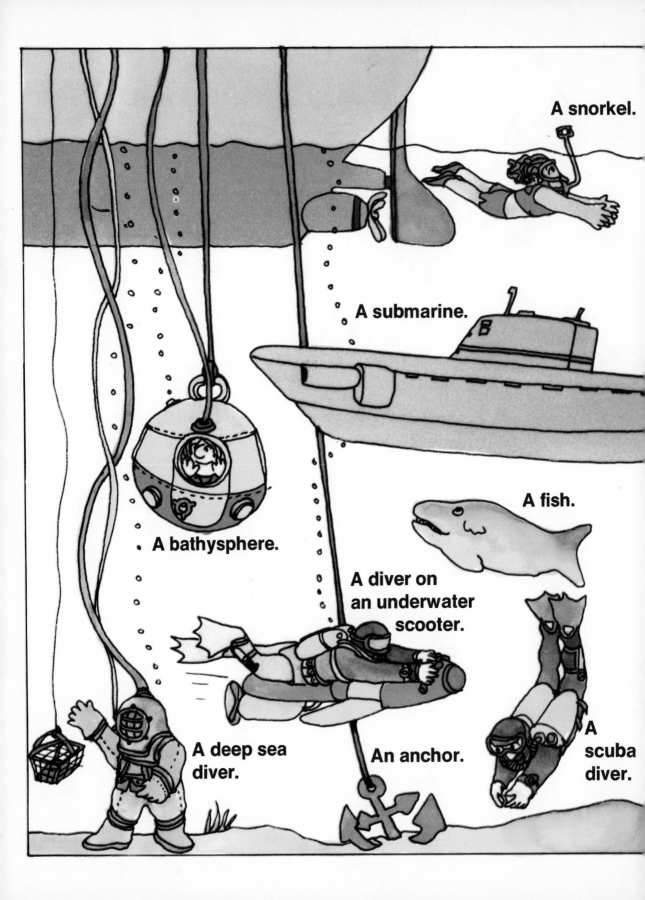

A snorkel.

A submarine.

A bathysphere.

A fish.

A diver on an underwater scooter.

A deep sea diver.

An anchor.

A scuba diver.

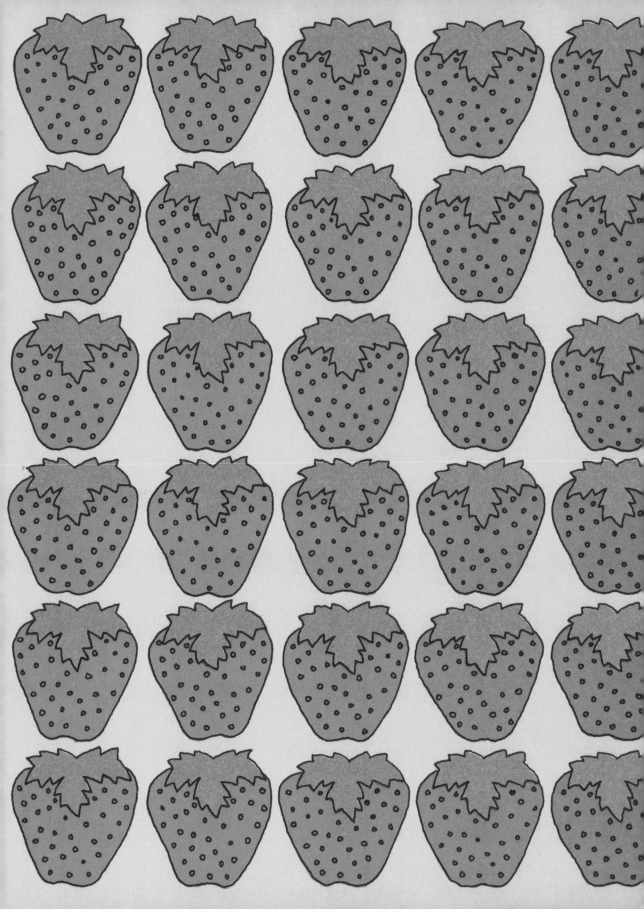